# IN THE BEGINNING
# THERE WAS NO SKY

A Story of Creation
Written by
## Walter Wangerin, Jr.

Illustrated by
## Joe Boddy

222

Thomas Nelson Publishers
Nashville • Camden • New York

Designed by Wayne Hanna of Hanna & Hanna, Inc.

In the Beginning There Was No Sky

Copyright © 1986 by Walter Wangerin, Jr.
Illustrations copyright © 1986 by Joe Boddy

Published in Nashville, Tennessee, by Thomas Nelson, Inc., and distributed in Canada by Lawson Falle, Ltd., Cambridge, Ontario.

Printed in the United States of America

ISBN 0-8407-6671-8

# IN THE BEGINNING

# THERE WAS NO SKY

Little child, do you know that I love you? With all my heart, I love you. Whenever you feel something, I feel it too. Did you know that? When you laugh, I smile. When you touch the caterpillar, I feel its bristling fur. And when you cry, I feel so sad, so sad, because I love you.

Yesterday I saw you crying. Your head was hanging down. Your bottom lip was trembling. You kept rubbing tears away with your two fists—and my heart nearly broke to see you. I don't want you to be sad. I felt like crying too.

Dear, dear child, why were you crying then? Do you remember? Were you lonely? Did you think that no one cared for you? Did you feel smaller than the caterpillar, lost in the grasses and forgotten?

Or were you scared? Did you think that something meant to hurt you—like a barking dog? Lightning and thunder? Or monsters?

Why were you crying? Maybe you were afraid of the dark. All of us are afraid in darkness sometime, because we feel so unprotected when we cannot see.

Come here, little child. Sit close to me, and do not cry. I love you. But God loves you even more than I do, and God knew that darkness could scare little children. Therefore, the first thing that he did in all the world was to make light. Did you know that? He said, "Let there be light"—and there was light, to chase the dark away.

But that was only the beginning of all the wonderful things that God did for the love of you. Oh, he performed marvels to keep you safe from fears and loneliness. Listen, listen to me, and learn why you don't need to cry.

In the beginning of time, even before this world was created, there was no sky. No sky—yes, that's a frightful thing to think about. It's like a room with no ceiling, like a house with no roof. If you had been here then, child, and if you had looked up in the daytime, you would have seen no clouds, no blue, just nothing at all. If you had looked up in the nighttime, you would have seen no stars, no moon, just empty spaces forever and forever.

No sky! What would protect you, my child, from the terrible emptiness of the universe when there was no sky above? Why, it would be like living in a nightmare all day long. Anything could happen. Creatures as strange as grasshoppers with human heads could swoop down to chase you, because there was no sky to stop them. And then you would be scared for sure, and no one would have blamed you if you cried.

But God knew that you'd be scared without a sky. And even in the beginning of time, the dear God was in love with you.

Therefore, after he made light and looked at the universe without a sky, the Lord God spoke. "No! No!" he cried in a voice like the clap of thunder. "This will never do," he said. "Soon I'm going to make a child. But first I must make a safe, protected space where my little child can live." And right away he went to work.

The great, good God stepped out on the rim of the universe, where only God can stand. Mighty was he, and unafraid of anything, and deep in love with you. He had a voice of tremendous power—and he was God.

"Nothing shall harm the child that I am going to make," he declared. "Nothing!" Then the Lord God raised his arm and swept it round from one side of the world to the other. "Let there be a roof here," he commanded. "Let there be a firm, blue dome to keep all frightful things from the world below." And God said, "Let there be a sky!"

And so it was: God made the sky as it is today, huge and high and comforting. He pricked its dark with tiny lights. He told the moon to ride at night, and the sun he sent to burn there in the daytime. He blew it full of wind and cloud. And he whispered, "For my child, to tell my child what time it is, and to guard my child at any time, day or night. Yes," said God as he looked up at his sky, "this is a good thing."

But as soon as God glanced down below the sky, he began to frown again. He saw a dreadful sight—something, child, you've never seen in all your life. He saw water, just water, vast and endless, rolling waters—nothing but waves on a deep green sea.

"No, no," he said, frowning. "This won't do either. If there's nothing but water in the world and not a place to stand on, my child would die."

Oh, child, can you imagine the danger, if you were living then? You'd be swimming in an ocean which flowed to the ends of the earth, so deep you couldn't find its bottom with your feet, so wide there wouldn't be a seashore anywhere. In all the world there would only be the sky, the sea, and you—swimming in the swelling waves. Soon you would grow tired. Then you would shout, "Help me! Help me!" But no one would answer. You would scream, "I am here! Is anybody there?" No—no one would be there but rolling water. So what could you do but cry? No one would blame you then. Or maybe you would just quit swimming, and sink down, and quietly wait to die.

But you don't have to cry, dear child, because God saw the danger of the water immediately. And remember: God was loving you already.

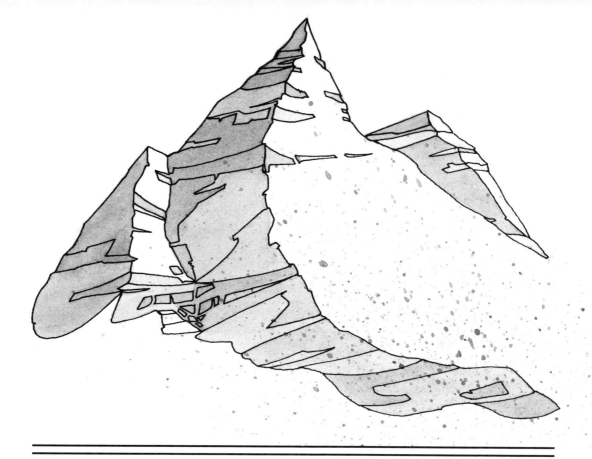

"The child I make should never fear, and shouldn't have to cry," God proclaimed. "The child I make shall have a place to stand on. I am the mighty God. I made protected spaces. Now I'll make the perfect place in which a child can live."

So God went to work again. He stood in the sky and roared to the ocean below, "Back, you waters! Go back till the dry land shows!" Then he blew on the water. His breath went out like the blasting of the storm wind. The ocean rolled backward in crashing waves, and the rocks rose up as cliffs to keep the oceans in their places. Land appeared—for you, my child. Mountains heaved upward. Can you imagine the rumble the mountains made when they were born? Water ran from their backs in streams and rivers. Some of the rivers filled the lakes. Some flowed to the oceans.

To the waters God said, "Now stay there forever." To the dry land he said, "Your name is the Earth." Then to himself he said, "But what is the best place for my child to live in?" And he smiled, "Why, the perfect place is a garden."

So God came down and plowed the land—for you, dear child. He planted the plains with a sweet green grass. He scattered flowers everywhere, simply to delight your eyes. He commanded the trees to stand up, to raise their branches in praise to Him and to shade you from the summer's sun.

"My child will have to eat," said God, and the ground grew beans and peas and beets and corn, the great, fat pumpkin, and broccoli: a vegetable garden. An orchard. To everything that grew he said, "Make seeds. Then let your seeds fall down to the ground so that something new is always growing. It's a hungry child I'm going to make, so give me food through all the years that my child can always eat."

It was a perfect place that God had made, a perfectly lovely garden and a good land.

But it was also perfectly silent, perfectly still, and for the third time God began to frown.

Dear child, nothing was moving in all that world. Nothing had eyes to look at you. Nothing had ears to hear you, nor faces for smiling. You could still cry out, "Hey! Hey! I am here! Is anybody there?" and not a creature would answer you. That perfect land was also perfectly lonely.

But the good God said, "I made the spaces. I made the perfect place. Now let me fill this place with music and with motion. I will make friends for my dear child."

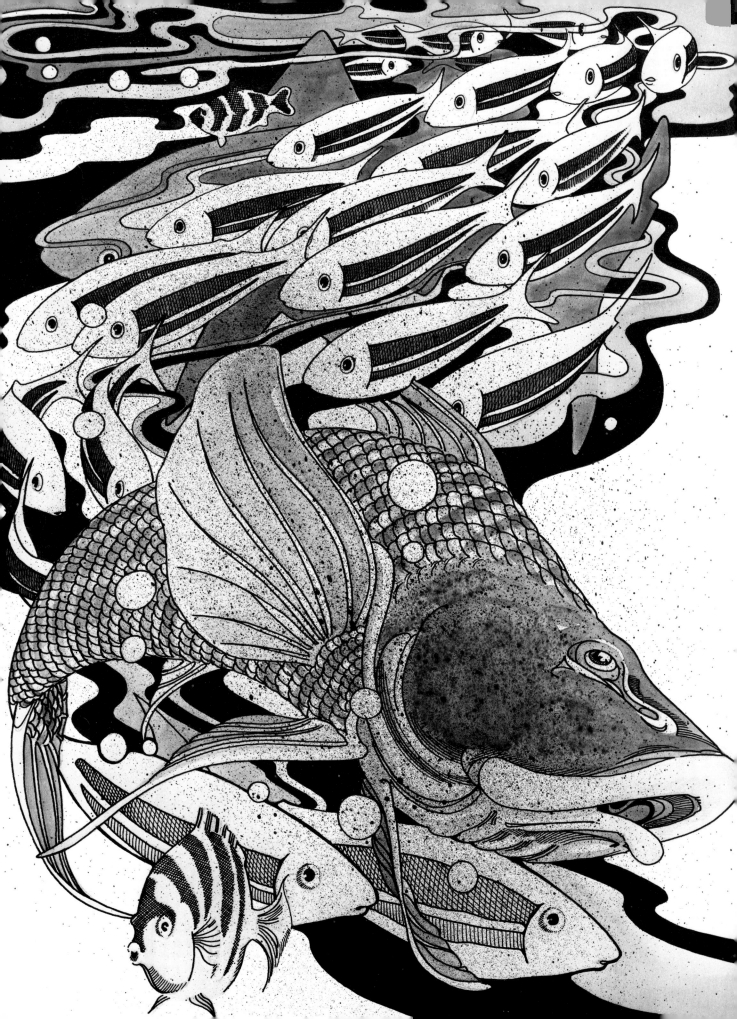

So the Lord God went to work again. He stood on the rock that rings the sea and uttered a strange new word. "Swarm!" he commanded, and the waters heard him. In the lakes there was a wriggling. In the rivers new shapes began to slither and flash. In the oceans huge forms darkened the deep, and some of them broke the surface with a mighty splash. So the fishes came to be.

Then God rose to ride the great, white clouds. He traveled from one corner of the heavens to another, roaring, "Swarm! Swarm!" And the heavens heard him. All at once there was a little song, a twittering, a sparrow hopping on stick feet. That sparrow sang for you, my child! Should you ever be lonely with sparrows about, singing the love of God? Then geese in long lines sailed the skies, trumpeting their gladness just to be. Swallows darted. Starlings clouded the air. The eagle frowned from crags in the mountain, and the hawk mounted the wind and wheeled.

Oh, child, you would have laughed to see such swimming and flying, to hear such choirs of music in the world—all for the love of God, and for you!

But still God wasn't done creating friends for you.

Now the mighty God came down and touched the soil, the dirt itself. He whispered, "Swarm," and the good earth heard him. It trembled and squeezed, and it bore its children. The caterpillars began to crawl, and ants and bugs and beetles.

Then animals came forth, my child, that walk the way you walk, on their feet; animals with hair like your hair, with noses, ears, and mouths that smile. They came two by two. They came in the thousands, and they filled the whole garden of the earth.

But every creature, as soon as it came, began to search for something.

The caterpillar twisted left and right, looking. The wolf cubs tumbled about sniffing for something. The lions and the leopards ran with smooth grace through the forests and the plains, looking, looking. The great bear stood on her legs and raised her nostrils to the wind, trying to find the scent of something important. But then she sat down sadly, because she couldn't find it. Something was missing! Lambs and goats, cows and oxen, birds and fish and all the beasts went wandering everywhere throughout the world, crying, "Where is it? Has anyone seen it?"

But no one found the thing that everyone desired, the thing which would finish creation, the most beautiful creature of all.

So the animals said, "Ask God." And that is exactly what they did.

Oh, child! This once in the whole history of the world all the living creatures came together in a single place. Ten thousand, thousand animals gathered at the mountains of God. They covered the hills and the valleys with life.

"Where?" they cried to the mighty God. "Where?" they pleaded in a million voices. "Where is the little child that shall lead us?"

God answered them quietly, "That child is not yet here."

And then it seemed that the mountains themselves burst into tears. But it was the sound of animals. Great and small, the animals were crying, child, exactly as I heard you crying yesterday, lonely and afraid—because without this child they could not even know their own names.

"Listen to me!" God made his voice sound like a trumpet, louder and clearer than their crying. "Listen to me," he called until the animals fell silent. Then he said, "Creation is ready now. The time is right. I have made the spaces. I have made a garden. I've filled my garden with goodness and music and friends. Now I shall make a child."

And then, dear child of mine, whom I love more than I can say—then God made you.

He descended to a valley where the earth was soft and good, an easy clay. The animals followed and sat in ranks up the sides of the valley, watching. The Lord God knelt beside a stream. He washed his hands and made them moist.

And then, while the multitude of animals held their breath, the dear God took clay and rolled and patted it. He worked it long and skillfully. Sometimes it looked as though he were knitting. Sometimes cutting cloth. Sometimes etching carefully, like a silversmith. Sometimes merely hugging, as a mother does her baby. Kneeling in the dirt, God gave that clay the length and weight and shape of a child.

All around him the animals were straining to see. And what did they see? A wonder none of them expected.

God himself was crying.

For when the clay had arms like your arms, child, and hands and fingers, when it had legs and feet and toes, then God leaned forward to make the face. And when the dear God leaned so far forward, tears dropped from his eyes to the little face below him.

The animals gasped. Why would God be crying? Was he sad or lonely? No, this is the reason: because he loved the face which he was making so very much that his heart was moved.

With his own tears, then, God polished the little face and its nose and its lips till they shined as brightly as his own. So there were two bright faces before each other. And one was God's, and one, my child, was yours.

God's eyes were open as he gazed at you. But your eyes were closed. You were a body, a marvelous, beautiful body. But you lay cold and still on the bank of the stream. You were not breathing. You were not alive.

Oh, God had put such wonders into that body: a heart, a mind, muscles and bones and a tongue. But the heart wasn't beating, and the tongue was still, and the mind was silent.

"Is this all?" the animals whispered. "Is this all the child will be? Just a lovely statue?"

But the Lord God Almighty was not yet done. He began to bow down farther than he'd ever bowed before—to you, my child. He brought his mouth closer and closer, until his lips touched your lips.

And then he kissed you. God kissed you. He breathed his own breath into you, so that your little lungs filled up with air, and color flushed all over your flesh, and a tingling went through you, and your heart bumped one great beat.

And you sneezed.

Well, that was such a surprise that God sat back and grinned.

You sneezed. Do you remember? Child, you had a fit of sneezing. Then your eyes flew open, and God's light entered into you, and you could see. And what was the first thing that you saw? You saw God. And he was laughing.

The great, good God was laughing with all his might at the sneezing child that he had made. It sounded to you like wonderful thunder. And all around you ten thousand animals were laughing too. They giggled and roared and bellowed. They cried, "Hurrah! Hosanna!" because the child that would lead them was alive. Oh, what a glorious music met you on that day, the day when you were made.

Then God reached toward you and touched your mouth. "This," he whispered, "can laugh and speak." He touched your breast. Do you remember the deep warmth of his touch? He said, "This can love. And these," he said, stroking your two good legs, "can run. Get up, child of God," he said. "Get up on your good legs, and run."

And that is exactly what you did. On green grass, under a strong blue sky, in the valley of the mountains of God, you leaped and laughed and ran the livelong day. The little beasts ran with you. The lion followed. The birds swooped low, singing a sweet song. And all the animals were friends of yours. You ate cherries when you were hungry. You drank a pure, clean water, unafraid of anything since everything was of the love of God for you. You grew happy, O my child. And when the evening came, why, you grew tired too.

And God knew that, as he had known everything else. God knew you were tired. So he made you a bed of rushes beside his stream. You lay down on that, and all the stars became your blanket, and the moon sent down her silver light.

"God?" you whispered.

He knelt down next to you. "What?" he asked.

And you said, "I'm so glad to be alive."

He smiled in the moonlight. You did too. It had been a very good day.

Just before you fell asleep, the dear God whispered, "Child, you must never forget that I love you. Do you hear me? I love you. I love you." He was stroking your hair as gently as the west wind does. He was touching your two eyes to close them lightly. He said, "Never, never, never stop loving me, my child. And to keep this love between us, " he whispered, "I give you everything that I have made. The earth, the sea, and the good green garden are yours to care for. The animals are yours to lead. They wait for you to give them names tomorrow."

"Even the caterpillar?" you said.

"Even the caterpillar," said God.

Then, as you slipped into your sleep, the Lord God murmured one last thing. "And this," he breathed, "shall be your name. Your name is _____."

And so it was God made you. He looked at everything that he had made, and said, "It's been a very good day." Yet when he looked on you, asleep beside his stream, he said, "But this child, this child is the best of all."

This is a true story, child. Tomorrow, go out and look at the world so you will see its truth; for there is the sky and the garden and the creatures the Lord God made for you. Will you feel lonely or sad or afraid again? Perhaps. And perhaps one day I'll tell you the story of why we feel such things, even though God loves us.

But for now, remember my story the next time tears run down your face. God himself can wipe those tears away.

And for now, sleep, sleep, my weary child, all peacefully—because you lie in the lap of God. And because I love you dearly.